MW00634347

The history of strategic airpower, the U.S. Air Force, and the U.S. aerospace industry are inexorably linked. For those in the industry, the desire to equip their fellow countrymen with the best the world had to offer drove innovation forward, from the use of balsa, to aluminum, to composites and from piston-powered props to jet engines. Over the course of nearly a century, the mission and aircraft have changed. But the quality and the character of the people have not changed. For generations, American men and women have answered their nation's call and served on the front line as airmen and within the aerospace industry, devoting their ingenuity, passion, energy, and in some cases their lives to this mission.

As we look toward the future, it is clear that men and women serving today, along with those in the aerospace industry, must remain united in the mission and deliver on the promise of strategic airpower for generations to come.

www.boeingstore.com

Printed in the United States of America.
First Printing June 2014

Permission to reproduce works of art, photographs, and artifacts in this volume was provided by the rights holders, when they could be identified. Every effort was made to obtain and verify accurate identifying information for the works. Please notify The Boeing Company of any inaccuracies, and corrections will be included in future editions.

ISBN: 978-0-9895977-8-4

Published by Boeing Press
www.boeingstore.com
For more information, please send an e-mail to customerservice@boeing.com.

Other titles available from Boeing Press:

Trailblazers: The Women of The Boeing Company
In Plane View: A Pictorial Tour of the Boeing Everett Factory
We Own the Night: The AH-64 Apache Story
The Jumbo Jet: Changing the World of Flight

Credits: Boeing would like to thank the many individuals who contributed their time and talents to this book, in particular the following: Writers: Michael Lombardi, Walt Rice. Designer: Cass Weaver. Editor: Bernadette Coleman. Photography: Boeing Historical Archives, Boeing Images.com, Lockheed Martin, with special thanks to Jeffrey Rhodes.

STRATEGIC AIRPOWER
THE HISTORY OF BOMBERS

FIRST EDITION   BY MICHAEL LOMBARDI   DESIGN BY CASS WEAVER

CONTENTS

THE CHAMPION OF FREEDOM FOR NEARLY A CENTURY, AMERICAN AIRPOWER WAS BORN FROM THE VISION, INGENUITY AND HARD WORK OF HUNDREDS OF THOUSANDS OF DEDICATED MEN AND WOMEN WHO HAVE SERVED THEIR COUNTRY DESIGNING, BUILDING, MAINTAINING AND FLYING AMERICA'S GREAT BOMBER AIRPLANES.

003	INTRODUCTION
005	VISION
017	FIRST BOMBER BUILDERS
029	A REVOLUTION IN STRUCTURES
043	BIRTH OF AMERICAN AIRPOWER
059	AMERICA GOES TO WAR
081	JET POWER
099	STRATEGIC AIR COMMAND
123	INNOVATION
147	THE MODERN TEST OF AIRPOWER

STRATEGIC AIRPOWER
THE HISTORY OF BOMBERS

Envisioning the Future

Strategic airpower began with men of vision. When William Boeing began his company in 1916, the airplane was considered a novelty, but Boeing saw a future in those frail structures of wood and fabric, a new technology that would be used to serve humankind—for travel, business, and to defend freedom. General William "Billy" Mitchell, a prophet of airpower, saw the airplane as the future of warfare and championed the cause of the strategic bomber and an independent Air Force—he is considered the father of the U.S. Air Force.

United in Mission

Boeing and Lockheed Martin have teamed throughout their histories, designing and building many iconic USAF bombers. It is a team that can trace its roots to the very beginning of flight. Aviation pioneer Glenn L. Martin sold William Boeing his first airplane, and Martin also gave Donald W. Douglas and North American Aviation founder James H. "Dutch" Kindelberger their start in the industry. During World War II, Boeing, Douglas, and Lockheed teamed to assemble Boeing B-17s, and Martin built Boeing B-29s. Most recently, Boeing and Lockheed teamed to build the world's premier air dominance fighter plane—the F-22 Raptor.

Driving Innovation

The history of U.S. bombers is the story of innovation. Bomber research and design has spurred on, or contributed to, some of the greatest advances in flight, including the transition of wood biplanes to all-metal monoplanes, aerial refueling, the world's first large swept-wing jet, and supersonic and hypersonic designs.

Arsenal of Democracy

Innovation is not limited to the design of bombers but is also a part of the manufacturing of those bombers. The production lines of the World War II "Arsenal of Democracy" built an incredible number of airplanes—Boeing and Lockheed Martin and their heritage companies, together built more than 159,000 airplanes for the war effort. One of the most innovative production systems was developed to build the highly complex B-29 Superfortress, and many of the practices and innovations from that time remain in use today.

Lasting Promise

William Boeing personally set the standard for quality when he started his company. While visiting his airplane fabrication shop at the Duwamish shipyard in 1916, Boeing saw a set of improperly sawed spruce ribs. He brushed them to the floor and walked all over them until they were broken. A frayed aileron cable caused him to remark, "I, for one, will close up shop rather than send out work of this kind." The Boeing promise to build the best planes possible for the airmen who fly them into combat has resulted in airplanes such as the B-17, legendary for its ruggedness and for saving its crews. The B-52 Stratofortress, famous for its longevity and mission flexibility, now more than 50 years old, is still at the tip of the U.S. airpower spear.

A Force for Freedom

Global airpower in the form of the strategic bomber ended hostilities and paved the way for democracy in World War II. It deterred aggression and defended the free world during the Cold War. Today, bombers continue to be on the front line, defending civilization and freedom. The success of U.S. strategic airpower is not just about airplanes; it is about people. It is the team of hard-working, dedicated, and very talented men and women, both those in the U.S. aerospace industry and their fellow Americans serving in the U.S. Air Force.

It was the fall of
1915, and in America
the science of flight
was falling behind.
The Wright Brothers
pioneered powered
flight, but little
progress had been
made in the United
States beyond that
milestone. Meanwhile
in Europe, the
airplane had been
enthusiastically
embraced, and
aviation technology
was accelerating at an
ever-increasing pace
as the Europeans,
locked in the Great
War, discovered the
military potential of the
airplane.

continued on page 6

STRATEGIC AIRPOWER
VISION

▲ In 1918, this was the front office for the Boeing Airplane Company, one of the many new buildings added to what would later be known as "Plant 1." The site was on the banks of the Duwamish River in South Seattle, formerly the Heath Shipyard that Bill Boeing purchased in 1910.

◀ William Boeing (right) with his pilot Eddie Hubbard stands on the ramp of the Boeing Airplane Company's boat house on Seattle's Lake Union after completing the first international airmail flight, flying mail from Vancouver, Canada, to Seattle, Washington, on March 3, 1919. This iconic photo conveys Boeing's pioneering spirit and enthusiasm for airplanes, which was so pervasive that even after a century it remains a fundamental part of the culture of The Boeing Company.

VISION

continued from page 5

On that European battlefield, long-range infantry rifles and machine guns had put an end to the cavalry charge and brought about the horrific bloody standoff of trench warfare.

But a new technology arrived in the skies over the trenches—structures of wood, fabric, and wire. Hardly what might be considered a weapon of war, they had buried in them the potential to eclipse

the role of the cavalry and revolutionize warfare in ways that only a few men of great vision such as Italy's great airpower theorist Giulio Douhet and Great Britain's airpower pioneer Hugh Trenchard were able to see at the time.

In America there were also men of vision who were not going to sit idly by and let the science of flight slip away. One of those men was William Boeing. As the son of German immigrants and having gone to school in Switzerland, he had a connection to Europe that made the news about the war all the more real to him. He watched with particular interest the advances of flight and the use of the airplane as a weapon, and he was disturbed by American complacency. He had his pilot, Herb Munter, take him up in his personal floatplane into the autumn

skies over Seattle to shower the city with cardboard bombs warning against the vulnerability of an unprepared United States.

The floatplane that Boeing flew was a Martin TA that he had purchased from fellow aviation pioneer Glenn Martin. Martin started his company in 1912 and ran it for the next 40 years—he was indeed the dean of aircraft manufacturers. Martin gave almost every great pioneer of aviation a start, including Donald Douglas, James S. McDonnell, and North American Aviation's founder Dutch Kindelberger. In a way Martin also gave Boeing his start; it was Martin's TA that inspired William Boeing to start his own airplane company on July 15, 1916.

Both companies made little impact on the war effort when America went "Over There" in April 1917, but it was the beginning of something grand. Today, 100 years after William Boeing bought that floatplane from Glenn Martin, the companies that still bear their names are the leading airplane companies in the world.

For Boeing, those were the first steps toward fulfilling his vision that airplanes would be more than a mere curiosity and that the technology of flight would serve America—both for transportation and defense. That vision led him to pioneer a commercial aviation infrastructure for America; unfortunately, it also led him to conflict with the U.S. Government.

Another visionary who would share the same fate as William Boeing was U.S. Army Brigadier General William "Billy" Mitchell. Mitchell had led the American air forces in Europe during World War I and was committed to his vision of an independent U.S. Air Force that could defend America's shores as well as project American airpower deep into an enemy's heartland. His passionate, sometimes overbearing, advocacy created many enemies and also led him into conflict with his own government. Both Boeing and Mitchell left the public scene under a cloud of controversy, but it would not be long before they were both exonerated and elevated to the status of pioneers of America's airpower—and the seeds they had sown did not take long to bear fruit.

On July 17, 1935, a gleaming four-engine monoplane bomber rolled out of the Boeing hangar at Boeing Field in Seattle. Boeing engineers simply called it the Model 299, but it was indeed the birth of American airpower. The Model 299, better known as the B-17 Flying Fortress, would make real Billy Mitchell's vision of airpower and fulfill William Boeing's vision of the airplane as a technology to defend freedom.

▲ The Boeing Company's first airplane was known as the B&W after the initials of William Boeing and his business partner, U.S. Navy officer George Conrad Westerveldt. The plane was based on the Martin TA that Boeing had purchased from Glenn Martin. Two B&Ws—named Bluebill and Mallard—were built. They were sold to the government of New Zealand in 1918.

▲ In 1917, the U.S. Navy ordered 50 Model C trainers from Boeing to support flight training of U.S. Navy pilots during World War I; it was Boeing's first government contract. This particular Model C is the C-700, bought by William Boeing for his private use.

▲ Boeing workers assemble Boeing Model C trainers on the company's first production line.

General View of Plant
Feb. 15 - 1919.

P-153

▲ Boeing "Plant 1," also known as the "Oxbow Plant," as it appeared in 1919. The taller building in the center back of the photo is the original Heath shipyard building that Boeing bought in 1910. Affectionately known as the "Red Barn," it is the birthplace of The Boeing Company. In 1975, the Red Barn was relocated to Boeing Field (King County International Airport), where it was meticulously restored and is now the centerpiece of the Museum of Flight.

SHARED HERITAGE. WILLIAM BOEING'S MARTIN TA TAXIS OUT ONTO SEATTLE'S LAKE WASHINGTON. BOEING HAD PURCHASED THE PLANE FROM FELLOW AVIATION PIONEER GLENN MARTIN. A CENTURY LATER, THE COMPANIES THEY FOUNDED CONTINUE AS TWO OF THE LARGEST AEROSPACE CORPORATIONS IN THE WORLD.

▲ Clockwise from top left. America's first home-built bombers, such as the Martin MB-2, were very similar in design to the Caproni.

Two of America's premier aviation pioneers: Glenn Martin (left) stands with Orville Wright.

Initially, the United States relied on British Handley Page and Italian Caproni bombers such as this Liberty engine-powered Ca-46.

American airpower was born in small shops where small groups of skilled craftsmen worked wood, shaped metal, and under the guidance of engineers, shop managers, and Air Corps technicians built America's first combat planes. In this December 1921 photo, Boeing employees and Air Corps representatives celebrate the completion of the GA-2. The GA-2 was a ground attack airplane designed by the U.S. Army Air Service Engineering Division (at that time it was fairly common for the Army to design its own airplanes or have one company design an airplane and then select another to build it). The skills developed in building the plane and the strong relationship that was formed between the Boeing Airplane Company and the U.S. Army became the foundation for a future of amazing accomplishments.

William Boeing wasn't America's only aviation pioneer. There were other young men whose imaginations were captured by the new science of flight, men like Donald Douglas and Dutch Kindelberger, who would start the great aviation companies Douglas Aircraft and North American Aviation. The one thing they had in common is that they got their start from Glenn Martin. In 1918 Martin received a contract to design and build the first American-built bomber. At the time, American airmen relied on the French-built Breguet 14 B.2 and British Airco DH.4 to serve as tactical bombers.

continued on page 18

STRATEGIC AIRPOWER
BUILDERS

▲ "Chicago" was one of the five Douglas World Cruisers. It and the "New Orleans" were the only planes to fly the entire around-the-world flight.

◀ Donald W. Douglas poses with one of his first airplanes—the DT. Based on the design of his first airplane, "The Cloudster," Douglas captured a U.S. Navy contract in 1921 to build the DT for the U.S. Navy, the first government contract for Douglas. The U.S. Army followed with an order for five derivatives of the DT to be used for the first around-the-world flight. They were known as Douglas World Cruisers (DWC).

BUILDERS

continued from page 17

The U.S. Air Service did not operate a U.S.-designed bomber similar to the British Handley Page, Italian Caproni, or German Gotha G.IV. Martin would remedy that by enlisting Douglas to design the new twin-engine bomber designated the MB-1.

An improved version of the MB-1, the MB-2, was made famous by Billy Mitchell when he set out to prove that airplanes could defend America's shores more effectively and cheaply than a fleet of U.S. combat ships. In his demonstration on July 21, 1921, bombs dropped from the MB-2 sank the captured German battleship *Ostfriesland* and, with it, the idea of the invincible battleship. This was a defining moment in airpower and naval history; no longer would naval battles be restricted to duels between surface fleets. In the future, airplanes would add a new deadly dimension to naval warfare.

After designing the MB-1, Douglas left Martin to start his own company, and it was not long before he gained success. His second design, the DT biplane torpedo bomber, was chosen by the U.S. Army Air Corps to be used in a special mission—the first around-the-world flight.

Known as the Douglas World Cruisers, four of these modified DTs named *Seattle, Boston, New Orleans*, and *Chicago* left Sand Point Airfield in Seattle on April 6, 1924. During the flight, the *Seattle* crashed in Alaska, and the *Boston* was forced down near the Faroe Islands. It was replaced by the *Boston II*, and the three planes completed the flight, returning to Seattle on September 28. The flight covered 23,942 nautical miles (44,342 kilometers) at an average speed of 70 mph and a total flying time of 371 hours, 11 minutes.

In another effort to draw attention, the fledgling USAAC set out to capture a record for endurance during a flight that began on January 1, 1929, by five USAAC pilots in a Fokker C-2 called the *Question*

Mark. The Fokker was refueled in mid-air from a Douglas C-1, which allowed the airplane to stay aloft for 150 hours while flying a circuit over Southern California—it was one of the pioneering efforts in using aerial refueling.

Although the flight of the *Question Mark* was solely for setting a record, Boeing did see a practical application for aerial refueling. In August of the same year, the Boeing Airplane Company partnered with the USAAC to conduct a transcontinental aerial refueling experiment to prove the practicality of in-flight refueling as a method to make nonstop transcontinental travel a reality.

To conduct this experiment, Boeing provided one of its newest mail plane designs, a Boeing Model 95 nicknamed the "Boeing Hornet Shuttle," as the endurance airplane. The pilots for the Boeing Hornet Shuttle were USAAC Captain Ira Eaker and Lieutenant Bernard Thompson.

Starting in Oakland, the Hornet Shuttle was refueled in-flight four times, arrived over New York after 28 hours and 25 minutes, and then returned to Oakland. Based on the flight, Eaker concluded that "the principle of transferring fuel in-flight will prove very important in certain military operations in the future." Twenty years later when the technology of aerial refueling was perfected, his words would prove to be prophetic.

While the Douglas World Cruisers and the early efforts at developing practical aerial refueling did not involve bomber airplanes, they did set the foundation for the concept of global reach, which would have a tremendous impact on the future of U.S. airpower, but before that concept could be realized, the Air Corps needed an airplane that amounted to a great leap beyond anything that had come before.

FORGOTTEN IN HISTORY. THE BOEING HORNET SHUTTLE, A MODIFIED BOEING MODEL 95 MAIL PLANE, WAS PART OF AN OPERATION THAT IS FORGOTTEN IN HISTORY. CHAMPIONED BY WILLIAM BOEING, WHO PARTNERED WITH THE ARMY AIR CORPS, THE PROJECT SUCCESSFULLY PROVED THE VIABILITY OF AERIAL REFUELING IN AN ACTUAL OPERATIONAL MISSION. U.S. ARMY AIR CORPS PILOT LIEUTENANT BERNARD THOMPSON, WHO SERVED AS COPILOT, POSES WITH THE BOEING HORNET SHUTTLE.

▲ On September 28, 1924, a jubilant Seattle crowd swarms the Douglas World Cruisers as they complete the first-ever around-the-world flight, which started and ended at Seattle's Sand Point Airfield.

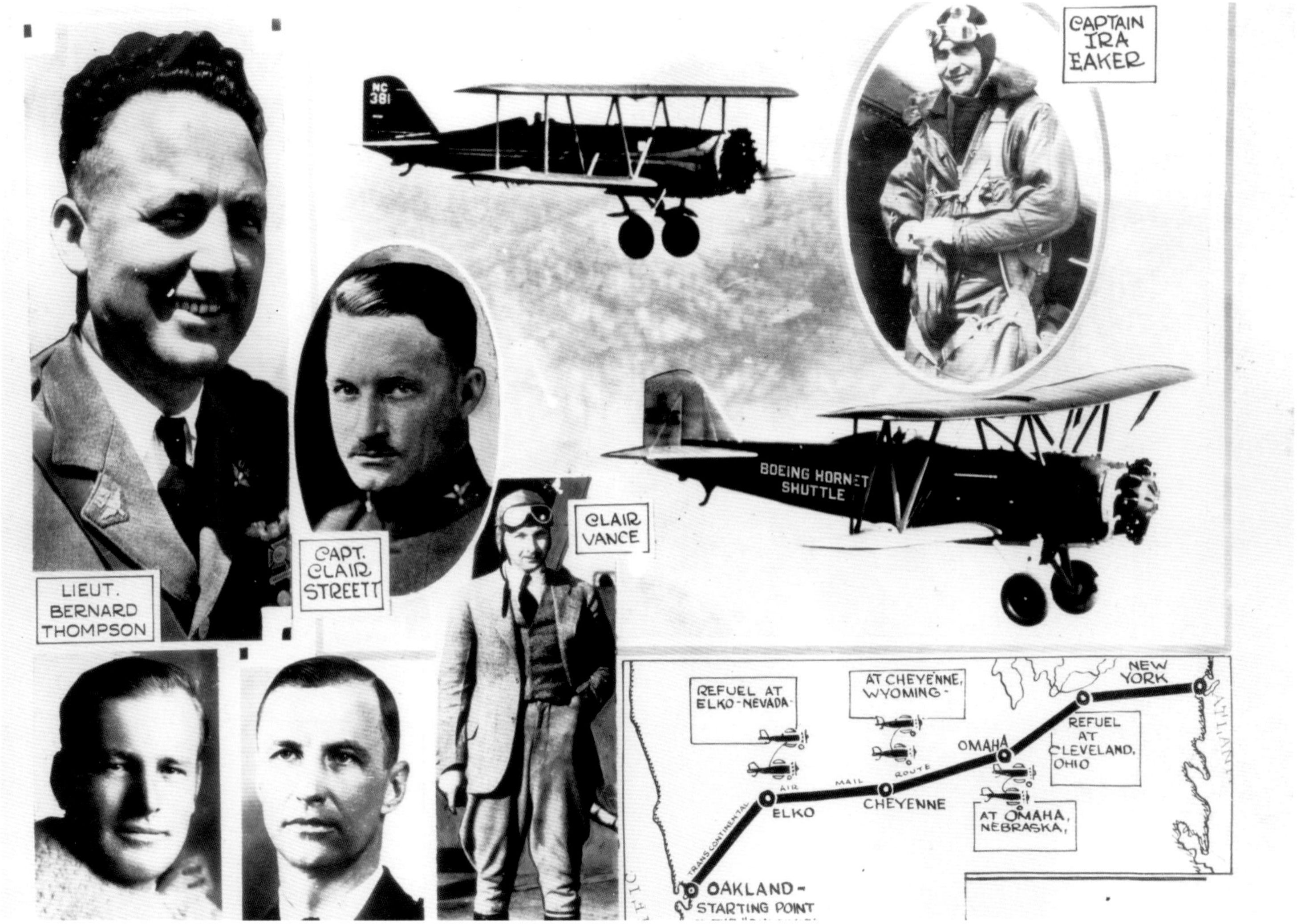
LIEUT. BERNARD THOMPSON
NC 381
CAPTAIN IRA EAKER
CAPT. CLAIR STREETT
CLAIR VANCE
BOEING HORNET SHUTTLE
REFUEL AT ELKO-NEVADA-
AT CHEYENNE, WYOMING-
NEW YORK
OMAHA
REFUEL AT CLEVELAND, OHIO
TRANS CONTINENTAL AIR MAIL ROUTE
ELKO
CHEYENNE
AT OMAHA, NEBRASKA,
OAKLAND - STARTING POINT

▲ This graphic shows the crews and the route flown by the Boeing Hornet Shuttle. Leaving Oakland on the morning of August 27, 1929, and after completing four aerial refuelings, the Hornet Shuttle reached New York after 28 hours and 25 minutes—and then returned to Oakland. Bill Boeing was looking for a way to make long-distance commercial flight viable, but the Air Corps pilot Ira Eaker saw the military potential: "The principle of transferring fuel in-flight will prove very important in certain military operations in the future."

AMERICA'S FIRST BOMBER. THE MARTIN MB-1, FIRST FLOWN ON AUGUST 17, 1918, WAS VERY SIMILAR TO ITALIAN CAPRONI AND BRITISH HANDLEY PAGE BOMBERS OF THE TIME.

▲ A young Donald Douglas (far right) got his start with Glenn Martin (second from right). As chief engineer, Douglas was the principal designer of America's first bomber, the MB-1. Martin also gave Lawrence Bell (left) his start. In 1935, Bell founded his own company—Bell Aircraft. Thomas Eric Springer (second from left) followed Douglas to Santa Monica and became the first test pilot for Douglas Aircraft.

▲ Dutch Kindelberger, a brilliant engineer and Air Corps pilot, also got his start in the aviation business with Glenn Martin. Kindelberger later joined Douglas Aircraft and was part of the design team that developed the DC-1, DC-2, and DC-3. He left Douglas to become the founder of North American Aviation (the manufacturing company), where he oversaw the design of legendary airplanes such as the P-51 Mustang, B-25 Mitchell, T-6 Texan, and F-86 Sabre. Very successful as the chief engineer of Douglas Aircraft, Dutch poses with a Douglas C-2 Army transport and his new Oldsmobile.

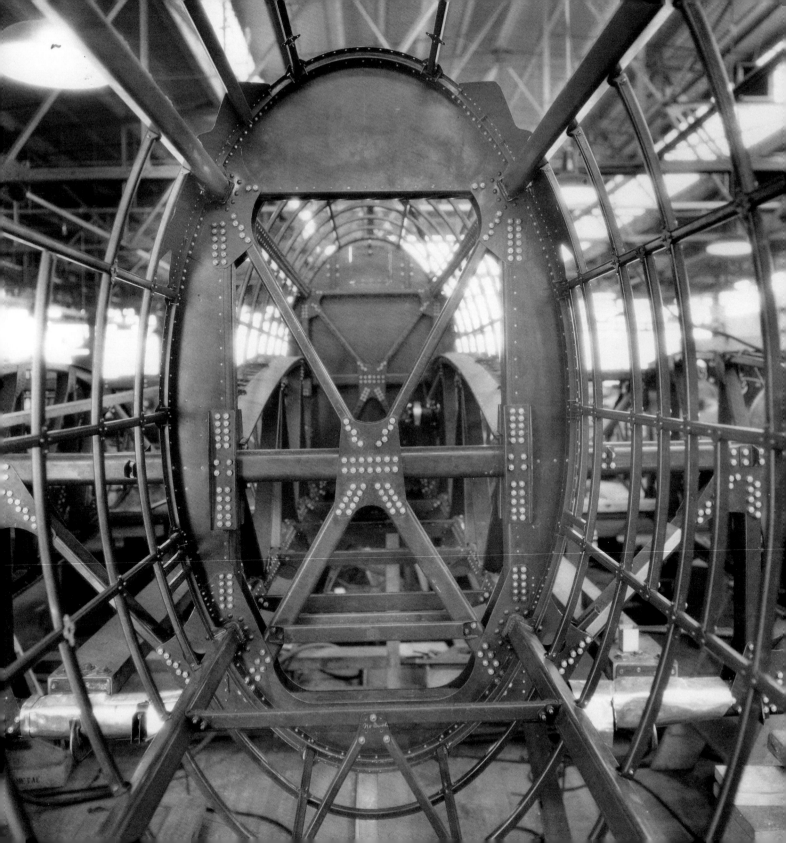

In 1915, Junkers pioneered all-metal construction with its J-1 transport, but the true revolution in airplane structures would not take place until 1930. It was the time of the Great Depression, and with meager budgets, the U.S. military could not drive advances in aviation. It was commercial aviation, boosted by the lucrative business of flying the air mail, that would drive the next evolution in aviation technology when biplanes made of wood and fabric finally gave way to metal frames and aluminum skin, and "streamlining" became the buzz word of airplane design.

continued on page 30

STRATEGIC AIRPOWER
REVOLUTION

▲ The Boeing Model 200 Monomail was a pioneer of all-metal monoplanes in the United States. Made completely of metal, it featured a streamlined, semimonocoque, fully cantilevered low-wing design. It also utilized retractable landing gear but still held onto the open cockpit—despite all of the new technology, pilots insisted that one needed to have the "wind in your face" to properly fly an airplane.

◀ Looking forward inside the fuselage frame of a Boeing B-9 is a view at a revolution in airplane structures that marked the transition from wood and fabric biplanes to all-metal monoplanes.

REVOLUTION

continued from page 29

The Boeing Airplane Company was an early pioneer in metal construction, having invented the arc-welded aluminum frame fuselages that the company used to replace the wood frame fuselages in DH-4s. In 1930, Boeing led the way with the airplane that marked the revolution to the all-metal monoplane with the Model 200 Monomail. While Boeing's competitors, Ford and Fokker, were building bigger tri-motor transports,

Boeing Chief Engineer Charles "Monty" Monteith felt that a smaller, faster transport that took advantage of the latest technology might be the way to go.

The smaller plane would be difficult to design and like many new ideas was not readily accepted, but doing the difficult and embracing new ideas followed the business philosophy of William Boeing, who declared in an interview that same year, "We have already proved that science and hard work can lick what appear to be insurmountable difficulties."

Boeing continued, "I've tried to make the men around me feel, as I do, that we are embarked as pioneers upon a new science and industry in which our problems are so new and unusual that

it behooves no one to dismiss any novel idea with the statement that 'it can't be done!'... Our job is to keep everlastingly at research and experiment, to let no new improvement in flying and flying equipment pass us by."

Monteith and his staff forged ahead into new territory and brought together all the latest technology possible into the design of the Monomail.

While Jack Northrop was developing a similar model in the Alpha, what made the Monomail unique was the combination the latest ideas of aeronautical design that included all-metal smooth-skin construction, as well as a semimonocoque fuselage, low-mounted cantilevered wings, an antidrag ring cowl, and most notably the first recorded use of retractable landing gear.

To the world of aviation, the Monomail defined the pattern that all future single-engine monoplanes would follow—including those that would be the frontline fighters of World War II. The technological experience gained from the Monomail led Boeing designers to the development of even more advanced twin-engine aircraft, including the B-9—America's first all-metal monoplane bomber—and the Model 247—the world's first modern commercial airplane.

While the B-9 was a milestone, it was merely an evolutionary airplane that still held onto the open-cockpit designs, and it was soon overshadowed by an even faster and more advanced design—the Martin B-10.

In 1933 the B-10 would earn Glenn Martin the highest recognition in U.S. aviation when President Franklin D. Roosevelt presented him with the Collier Trophy.

Two years later an improved version of the B-10, known as the Model 146, was sent to Wright Field to compete against Boeing and Douglas for the next Air Corps bomber contract. Unfortunately for the B-10, the rapid pace of technology had already passed it by.

▲ Boeing had been an early pioneer in metal. Here, new all-metal fuselage frames are being manufactured at Boeing Plant 1 to replace the wood frames in U.S. Army DH-4s. To join the metal frames, Boeing invented electric arc-welding. Boeing rebuilt 298 of the British-designed bombers between 1920 and 1925. It is interesting to note that although Boeing had ready access to inexpensive airplane-grade spruce from his own timber holdings, he still chose to go forward with metal construction.

By 1933, the Boeing plant was fully turned over to all-metal airplanes. Here the Model 247, the world's first modern airliner, is being assembled alongside P-26 fighter planes—America's first all-metal monoplane fighters.

POISED AND READY. A BOEING-BUILT DH-4M ON THE SANDLOT FIELD NEAR BOEING PLANT 1.

▲ A later version of the Monomail, eight feet longer than the earlier Model 200, the Boeing Model 221 was designed to carry passengers rather than as pure mail plane. Technology was accelerating at such a rapid pace that even though the Monomail was a pioneer for the all-metal monoplane, it was quickly eclipsed by the Boeing 247, and only the two were built. The performance potential of the clean airframe of the Monomail did inspire advances in engines as well as the design of the variable-pitch propeller.

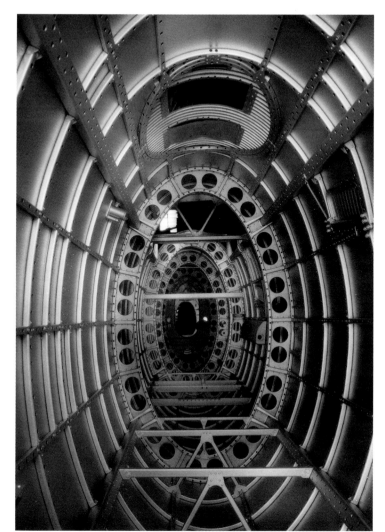

⏴ Clockwise from top left. The abstract beauty of the interior of a newly completed Y1B-9A emphasizes the artistry inherent in great engineering.

Monomial technology was quickly adapted to military use, and Boeing submitted the all-metal YB-9 to the U.S. Army Air Corps. The Army bought two prototypes and five Y1B-9As.

Fokker competed against the B-9 with its XB-8. With wings made of wood and fabric-covered fuselage, it lagged behind the Boeing plane in technology and was not selected as a bomber. The Army did take seven of the planes as O-27 observation airplanes.

OFF THE LINE. A NEWLY ASSEMBLED Y1B-9A AT BOEING FIELD, JULY 1932.

▲ The Douglas Y1B-7 was also a contemporary of the B-8 and B-9. Seven were built, along with five similar Y1O-35 observation airplanes.

▲ Just as the Monomail was quickly replaced by the 247, the Martin B-10 limited the production of the Boeing B-9 and Douglas B-7.

In 1934, the Roosevelt administration had forced the breakup of William Boeing's United Aircraft and Transport Corporation. The breakup created three separate companies: United Aircraft (United Technologies), United Airlines, and the Boeing Airplane Company along with Wichita's Stearman Aircraft, which Boeing inherited as part of the breakup. The Boeing Airplane Company found itself alone at a time of increasing competition in its bread-and-butter fighter plane market and was also looking at being shut out of the commercial airplane market with the introduction of the Douglas DC-2 and DC-3.

continued on page 44

STRATEGIC AIRPOWER
BIRTH

▲ A pair of B-17Ds wait for predelivery flight-testing on the Boeing flight ramp at Boeing Field in Seattle.

◀ A Boeing mechanic works on the inboard engine of a B-17D.

BIRTH
continued from page 43

With the breakup also came news of the retirement of William Boeing, the company's inspirational founder. Fortunately, Boeing had a good eye for talent and left his company in the hands of excellent leadership. To manage his airplane company, Boeing selected Claire Egtvedt. Egtvedt had already led the company into metal monoplanes and knew that the company was well-positioned to follow him into a bold new direction of designing and building large airplanes: the "Big Boeings." It was one of the most important decisions in business history; 80 years later, The Boeing Company continues to be the world leader in the design and manufacture of large airplanes.

In August 1934, Air Corps Circular 35-26 invited Boeing to compete on a new airplane described as "bombardment, multiengined." Designers "Monty" Monteith, Robert Minshall, E. G. Emery, and a young Ed Wells took the visionary step of interpreting the Air Corps' "multi-engined" to be four engines rather than the standard two-engine design. Under Egtvedt's direction, $432,034, almost the entire cash reserve of the Boeing Airplane Company, was allocated to build a four-engine bomber prototype. It was a tremendous risk; if the plane was not accepted, it is likely that Boeing would not have survived the Depression.

Rolling out of the Boeing hangar simply as Boeing "Model 299," *Seattle Times* reporter Richard Smith dubbed the new plane a "Flying Fortress," a name that Boeing quickly adopted and trademarked. On July 28, 1935, Boeing test pilot Les Tower took the 299 up from Boeing Field for its first flight and later made a record-breaking flight from Seattle to Wright Field in Dayton, Ohio, where the airplane was to fly off against its competition, the Douglas B-18. Tragically, an accident during the flyoff killed Tower and Air Corps pilot Major Ployer Pete Hill and destroyed the 299.

The accident knocked Boeing out of the bomber competition, which was then won by the Douglas B-18, but the Model 299 had impressed the Air Corps so much that discretionary funds were used to ensure that the plane would be built.

On January 17, 1936, Boeing received an order for 13 Y1B-17 service test airplanes, vindicating Egtvedt's gamble and cementing his legacy as the father of the Flying Fortress. The B-17 would also vindicate Billy Mitchell; now the Air Corps had an airplane that would make real his vision of airpower. Tragically, Mitchell did not live to see it unfold; he passed away just one month after the order for the B-17.

After receiving the first Flying Fortresses in May 1937, the Air Corps put them into action in a joint Army–Navy exercise near San Francisco, where the B-17s located and scored hits on the battleship USS Utah using water bombs.

In February 1938, six B-17s flew to Argentina, leaving from Miami and landing in Buenos Aires. Not only was it a goodwill flight but also a proof of the long-range capability of the new bomber.

On May 12, 1938, three B-17s guided by a young navigator, Curtis LeMay, located and photographed the Italian luxury liner Rex in a highly publicized interception that occurred 620 nautical miles off the coast of New Jersey in a heavy overcast. After a backlash from the event, President Roosevelt stepped in and personally ordered the expansion of the Air Corps to defend the Western Hemisphere. The B-17s' outstanding performance in naval interception and long-range flight had done the job of making both the president and future Army Chief of Staff George C. Marshall believers in long-range airpower.

At Boeing, the company did not have room to build the new bombers and broke ground for a new factory at Seattle's Boeing Field on May 15, 1936; by November, assembly of the Y1B-17s was moved to the site. The finished building, known as Plant 2, was not much larger than a football field at 200 feet wide and 300 feet deep, but it was big enough to hold nine B-17s. Over the next five years, Plant 2 would be expanded three more times, and by 1941 it was one of the most modern airplane manufacturing sites in the world, covering 1,776,000 square feet—it was called Boeing's "Fortress Factory," and it was ready to mass-produce Flying Fortresses when war came to America on December 7, 1941.

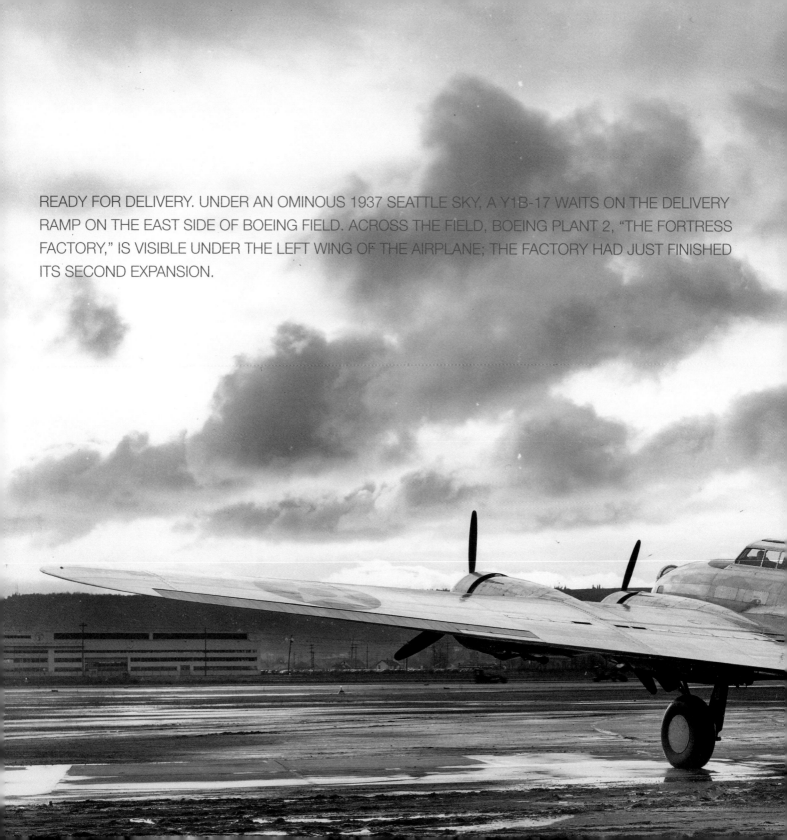

READY FOR DELIVERY. UNDER AN OMINOUS 1937 SEATTLE SKY, A Y1B-17 WAITS ON THE DELIVERY RAMP ON THE EAST SIDE OF BOEING FIELD. ACROSS THE FIELD, BOEING PLANT 2, "THE FORTRESS FACTORY," IS VISIBLE UNDER THE LEFT WING OF THE AIRPLANE; THE FACTORY HAD JUST FINISHED ITS SECOND EXPANSION.

⏶ Completed in December 1936, North American Aviation's XB-21 competed against the Douglas B-18. While the XB-21 had better performance, NAA priced it at twice the cost of the Douglas plane. With a limited budget, the Air Corps went with the B-18. The XB-21 gave NAA experience in building twin-engine bombers, which paid off well just four years later when NAA introduced the excellent B-25.

▲ In mid-1939, B-17Bs and Model 307 Stratoliners crowd the interior of Boeing's new plant at Boeing Field known as "Plant 2." Within a year, the factory would be expanded again and busy building Douglas DB-7 (A-20C) bombers for the Allies.

▲ B-17Cs at the Boeing hangar on the east side of Boeing Field. The B-17C first flew on July 21, 1940.

▲ Clockwise from top left. First flown on October 15, 1937, the Boeing XB-15 was a testbed for very large long-range bombers, with a range of more than 5,000 miles and a wingspan of 150 feet.

The Douglas XB-19 was part of the same program as the XB-15 but flew much later in June 27, 1941. It had a range of 7,900 miles and a wingspan of 212 feet.

The Douglas B-18 production line at Santa Monica, California.

A Y1B-17 flies over Washington, DC.

FIRST APPEARANCE. ON JULY 17, 1935, BOEING INTRODUCED THE MODEL 299 TO THE PUBLIC. SEATTLE NEWSPAPER REPORTER RICHARD SMITH DESCRIBED IT AS A "FLYING FORTRESS," A NAME THAT BOEING ADOPTED.

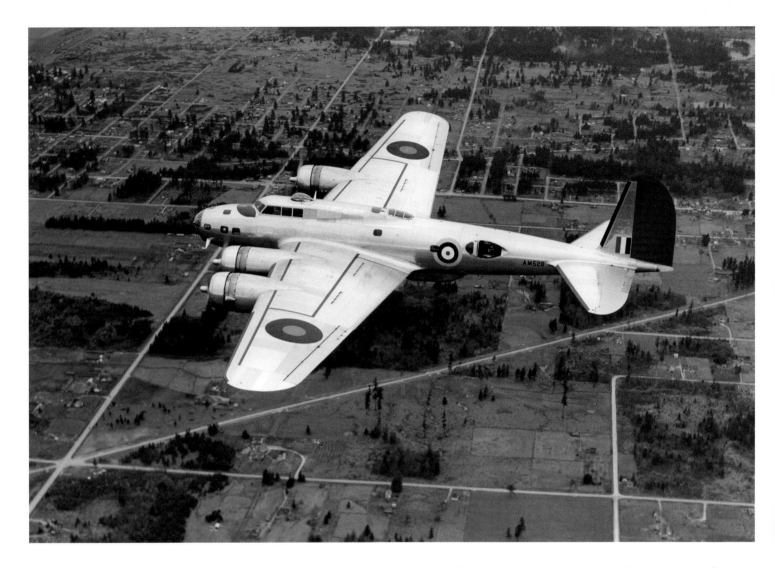

▲ A B-17C built for the Royal Air Force: Great Britain was the first to fly the Fortress into combat in Europe and found some weaknesses with the airplane that Boeing was able to correct beginning with the B-17E.

▲ An in-flight view of the XB-15: The wing of the giant bomber was so large that the flight engineer could access the engines for small repairs from inside the wing. The same wing would later be used on the Boeing 314 Clipper.

STREAMLINED. A B-17C SHOWS THE BEAUTIFUL CLEAN LINES OF THE
MODEL 299 FAMILY.

Many historians credit the Allied victory in World War II to a number of key factors, including the development of a worldwide logistics system necessary to fight a global war, the fighting prowess of the troops, the command ability of a certain leader, or the superiority of some specific weapon. While these are undeniably important to the victory, it can also be said that America and her allies simply out-produced Germany and Japan. It was a victory that began on the home front—the "Arsenal of Democracy"—and one of the key ingredients was teamwork.

continued on page 60

STRATEGIC AIRPOWER
GOES TO WAR

▲ In a photo that says "airpower," B-17Fs of the 95th Bomb Group, part of the "Mighty Eighth" Air Force based in England, head out on a mission. The 95th had the distinction of being the first bomb group to fly a mission to Berlin.

◀ B-17Gs on the production line at the Douglas Long Beach plant. Douglas and Lockheed Vega teamed with Boeing to build the B-17F and G.

GOES TO WAR

continued from page 59

It was a team effort between industry and government, setting aside differences and paving the way for unfettered production. It was a team effort among industry, unions, local government, and the media to recruit workers, especially women into the nontraditional role of working in a factory or shipyard. Even rival airplane manufacturers set aside competition and teamed together to build each other's airplanes.

One of the first such teaming efforts involved Boeing, building under license Douglas DB-7Bs for France and Great Britain as part of a joint Boeing/Douglas effort. Boeing and Douglas continued to work together and also brought Lockheed

(Vega) into the joint production team called the BDV committee (Boeing, Douglas, Vega). Together, the team built 3,405 B-17Fs and 8,680 B-17Gs between 1943 and 1945. The Consolidated B-24 Liberator became the most produced heavy bomber of the war and the most produced airplane in the United States, with 18,482 built by a team of four manufacturers: Consolidated, Ford, Douglas, and North American Aviation.

The Boeing B-29 Superfortress was built in Renton, Washington, and Wichita, Kansas, by Boeing; by Martin in Omaha, Nebraska; and by Bell in Marietta, Georgia, in a plant now operated by Lockheed Martin. The innovative production system developed for the B-29 was one of the most advanced in the world. Even though the B-29 was arguably the most technologically complex airplane of the war, Boeing workers in Renton were able to build 160 of the giant airplanes in one month, and many of the innovations that made this possible are still in use

today. These bombers were guided by the architect of America's global airpower strategy, General Henry Harley "Hap" Arnold. Under Arnold, the modern U.S. Air Force was born.

In Europe, flying at night, Royal Air Force bombers had already begun their own strategic air campaign against Hitler's Third Reich. Starting in January 1943, American bombers joined the campaign, flying into Germany by day. These missions were flown by the men of the "Mighty Eighth" and the 15th Air Forces. Their valor has become the stuff of legend. Flying B-17 Flying Fortresses and B-24 Liberators, they flew up to 50 missions into the heart of the enemy's homeland, with only heated flight suits and oxygen masks to protect them from an environment similar to that at the top of Mt. Everest. They faced an even greater danger from the expert pilots of the German Luftwaffe and some of the heaviest anti-aircraft fire in history, all determined to destroy the American bombers.

The sacrifice was tremendous; the air war in Europe claimed the lives of tens of thousands of Allied fighter and bomber crews. The Allied bombers attacked aircraft factories and petroleum supplies. The Luftwaffe was forced to redirect its planes from the support of German ground forces to the defense of the German homeland, and the attrition of the constant air battles over France and Germany left the Luftwaffe with just 80 airplanes available to face the thousands of Allied planes over Normandy on June 6, 1944. In those deadly skies, the B-17 earned a lasting reputation for being stable and rugged; there are volumes of stories of Flying Fortresses that returned their crews safely to their bases so badly damaged that the planes never flew again, earning the unending affection of her crews—to them the airplane was the "Queen of the Skies."

The B-17 became an icon of American airpower. General Carl Spaatz, the American air commander in Europe, stated it simply: "Without the B-17, we might have lost the war."

In the Pacific, airpower both from island airbases and from the decks of carriers drove back the Japanese. A medium bomber designed for a tactical role conducted one of the most strategic attacks of the war; on April 18, 1942, in one of history's most effective and audacious uses of airpower, General James H. Doolittle led 16 B-25 Mitchell bombers from the deck of the U.S. aircraft carrier USS *Hornet* and struck targets in Tokyo. The actual damage was nominal, but the effect on morale for America and Japan was immeasurable. B-25s also proved their strategic value through the interdiction of Japan's shipping lanes, cutting off the flow of vital strategic materials and oil. B-25G and H models armed with a 75-mm cannon and later B-25Js with up to 14 .50-caliber machine guns devastated Japanese shipping and accounted for more tonnage sunk than U.S. Navy submarines.

The most important bomber of World War II, the B-29 Superfortress was the most expensive program of the war

and quite possibly the most advanced technologically (even considering the Manhattan Project that built the atomic bomb). In the end, the B-29 proved its value. The USAAF, relying on the Superfortresses, conducted a strategic bombing campaign that crippled Japan's war-making capability. In August 1945, B-29s dropped atomic bombs on the Japanese cities of Hiroshima and Nagasaki, and within days Imperial Japan surrendered unconditionally. Airpower had brought the global war to an end.

Throughout the war, the quality of pilots and planes accounted for much, but in the end it was quantity that played a major role in victory. American workers building the "Arsenal of Democracy" had vastly out-produced the Axis, building a total of 296,000 aircraft during the war. In 1944 alone, America produced 95,272 aircraft, two and half times more than Germany's production of 39,807 for the same year, and more than Japan's entire war production of 65,300 aircraft.

EN ROUTE. STREAMING CONTRAILS FOLLOW THESE 2ND BOMB GROUP B-17GS AS THEY HEAD OVER THE ALPS. THE 2ND BOMB GROUP WAS BASED NEAR FOGGIA, ITALY, AND WAS PART OF THE U.S. 15TH AIR FORCE.

▲ Clockwise from top left. The Consolidated B-32 Dominator was built to supplement the B-29 Superfortress. Arriving at the end of the war, it had a very short production run, and only 118 were built. The Dominator had the distinction of being the last Allied airplane to see combat in World War II.

The Consolidated B-24 line at Fort Worth, Texas: In the foreground are transport versions of the B-24 known as the C-87. The flag-draped airplane is the last C-87 built. On the left side of the photo are B-24J Liberator VIs for the Royal Air Force Coastal Command.

This B-17 is the last flyable B-17F in the world. It was restored by The Boeing Company and is part of the collection of the Museum of Flight in Seattle.

The B-24 was the most produced U.S. airplane during World War II. It served along with the B-17s in Europe and also served in the South Pacific. Here, B-24Js fresh off the production line at North American Aviation's Dallas plant wait for delivery on the flight line. NAA built 966 of the Consolidated-designed B-24G and Js.

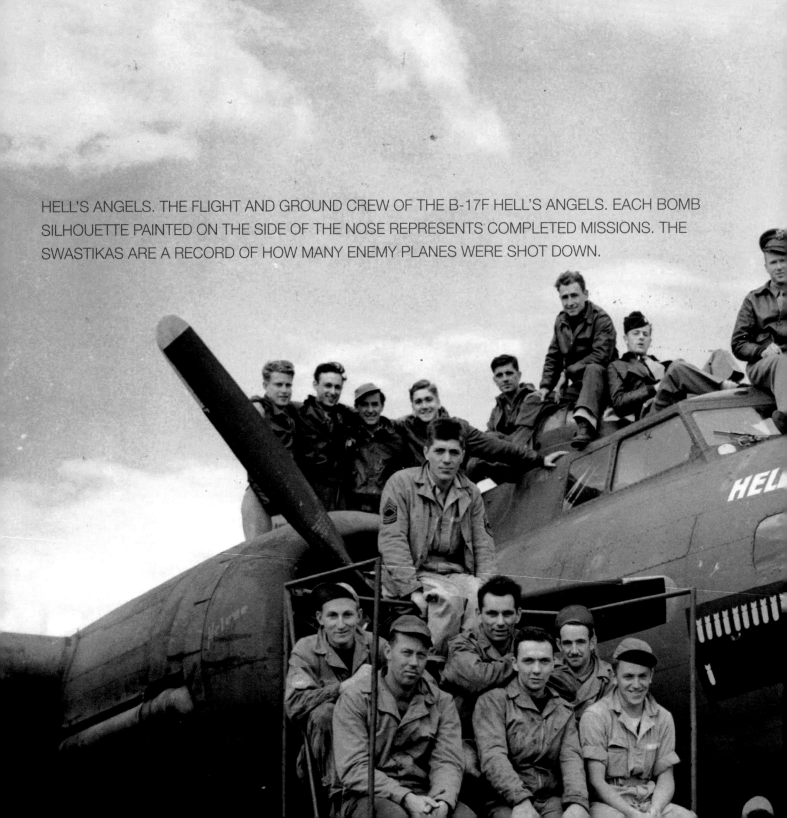

HELL'S ANGELS. THE FLIGHT AND GROUND CREW OF THE B-17F HELL'S ANGELS. EACH BOMB SILHOUETTE PAINTED ON THE SIDE OF THE NOSE REPRESENTS COMPLETED MISSIONS. THE SWASTIKAS ARE A RECORD OF HOW MANY ENEMY PLANES WERE SHOT DOWN.

▲ Clockwise from top left. The architect of America's global air war strategy, General Henry "Hap" Arnold, meets with aviation pioneer William Boeing, who returned to The Boeing Company as an advisor during the war.

March 31, 1944: The final B-17 built during the month of March rolls off the line, setting a record of 362 B-17s built in one month at the Boeing plant in Seattle.

To protect airplane plants on the West Coast from the possibility of Japanese carrier attacks such as the one at Pearl Harbor, the plants were painted as well as covered in a camouflage made of chicken wire, burlap, and plywood that mimicked the surrounding neighborhood, including houses and automobiles.

Women workers, who proudly went by the moniker "Rosie the Riveter," made up nearly half the workforce in most aviation plants during the war. Here, Boeing Rosies install the waist gun mounts in a B-17.

▲ In May 1944, Boeing rolled out the 5,000th B-17 built by the company since America's entry into World War II. The airplane is covered with the names of the employees who built the airplane—a practice that became commonplace throughout the aviation industry whenever a milestone airplane was rolled out.

▲ The first of the big-tail B-17s: The first B-17E is shown on its first flight on September 5, 1941. Five hundred and twelve were built.

▲ Rosies in the Pacific Northwest numbered in the thousands, recruited by posters that said rivet work was easy—just like pinning a pattern on fabric to make a dress. Rosies helped boost airplane production at The Boeing Company from 60 per month in 1942 to an astounding 362 per month by March 1944. At one point, the Seattle plant rolled out 16 B-17 bombers in 24 hours. Boeing assisted working moms in locating day care and providing work shifts that would allow mothers to be at home during the day.

ROLE PLAYER. THE NORTH AMERICAN AVIATION B-25H MITCHELL, NAMED FOR AIR FORCE PIONEER BILLY MITCHELL, WAS A MEDIUM BOMBER THAT PLAYED A NUMBER OF VERY IMPORTANT STRATEGIC ROLES. IN THIS GUNSHIP CONFIGURATION, IT COULD ATTACK A TARGET WITH 10 .50-CALIBER MACHINE GUNS AND A 75-MM CANNON—THE SAME GUN USED ON THE M-4 SHERMAN TANK.

▲ B-25H, "Bones," was the 1,000th and last B-25H built as well as the last B-25 built at NAA's Los Angeles plant. Like other milestone airplanes, it was signed by the employees who had assembled the plane. North American Aviation continued to build B-25s at its plant in Kansas, where all B-25J models were built.

⏶ Between its completion in March and fly-away on April 15, 1945, almost every employee group at the Martin Baltimore plant took turns posing in front of the last Marauder, a B-26G-25 called "Tail End Charlie "30."" "30" is a traditional mark in news articles denoting the end of a story.

The Douglas A-26 Invader was a follow-on to the Douglas A-20, replacing that plane as well as the NAA B-25 and the Martin B-26. In June 1948, the USAF dropped the "A" for attack designation, and the A-26 became the B-26. It served in World War II, Korea, and Vietnam.

DYNAMIC ADDITION. THE UNITED STATES WAS FULLY COMMITTED TO AIRPOWER, AND THE B-29 ALONG WITH THE MANHATTAN ATOMIC WEAPONS PROJECT WERE AMERICA'S NUMBER ONE WARTIME PROGRAMS. EVEN THOUGH THE B-29 WAS ARGUABLY THE MOST TECHNOLOGICALLY ADVANCED AIRPLANE OF THE WAR AND BUILT ON ONE OF THE MOST ADVANCED PRODUCTION LINES EVER, BOEING GAVE A MAXIMUM EFFORT AND WAS ABLE TO MOVE THE PLANE QUICKLY FROM CONCEPT TO THE FRONT LINE. PRODUCTION ENGINEERING BEGAN ON JUNE 6, 1941, AND THREE YEARS LATER ON JUNE 5, 1944, B-29S FLEW THEIR FIRST COMBAT MISSION.

THE EFFORT WAS NOT WITHOUT COST. THE HUMAN TOLL FOR BOEING WAS TREMENDOUS, INCLUDING THE LOSS OF FAMED TEST PILOT EDDIE ALLEN AND HIS FLIGHT-TEST CREW IN AN ACCIDENT THAT DESTROYED ONE OF THE XB-29 TEST AIRPLANES. LATER, THE STRAIN OF MANAGING THE MASS PRODUCTION OF THE SUPERFORTRESS WOULD CLAIM THE LIFE OF THE BOEING COMPANY'S BELOVED PRESIDENT AND ARCHITECT OF MASS PRODUCTION PHILIP JOHNSON, WHO SUFFERED A STROKE WHILE INSPECTING THE B-29 LINE IN WICHITA.

▲ The B-29 was the first mass-produced combat airplane to have a pressurized cabin. Unlike the crews on the B-17 and the B-24 who bundled up in heated flight suits and leather flight jackets, the crews in the B-29 could fly in their shirtsleeves.

▲ Clockwise from top left. Wing and body join on the Boeing Wichita B-29 line. The modular design of the B-29 was one of the vital aspects of the airplane's assembly, allowing the highly complex planes to be built at rates greater than 100 airplanes per month.

The B-29 assembly at Boeing Renton consisted of four assembly lines that moved at a continuous rate.

At Renton, production increased quickly from two airplanes in January 1944 to 160 in July 1945—an average of five giant bombers built each workday.

The B-29 wing line at Boeing in Renton, Washington: Nineteen stations of wings were mounted on rails and moved along at specified times. When moving, the wings would travel at six feet per minute.

The invention of the jet engine and subsequent jet-powered aircraft came about almost simultaneously and independently in both England and Germany. A Royal Air Force cadet, Frank Whittle, submitted the first patent for a jet engine in 1930 and had a working engine in April 1937. Unaware of Whittle's work, Hans von Ohain began work on his own jet engine in Germany and had a running engine in September 1937. A Heinkel 178 airframe powered by Ohain's engine became the world's first jet airplane when it flew on August 27, 1939.

continued on page 82

STRATEGIC AIRPOWER
JET POWER

▲ The XB-47 rolls out of Boeing Plant 2 in Seattle on September 12, 1947—the first of 2,032 B-47s.

◀ The Boeing B-47 was a radical design that pioneered the combination of swept wings and podded engines—its design is still the basic pattern for large subsonic jets built today, including all those made by Boeing and Airbus.

JET POWER

continued from page 81

On May 15, 1941, the British followed with their first jet, the Whittle-powered Gloster E.28/39. Both countries had jet airplanes that were used in combat during World War II, notably Britain's Gloster Meteor and Germany's Messerschmitt Me 262. Germany also introduced the world's first operational jet-powered bomber, the Arado Ar 234.

In America, jet research lagged well behind the work being done in Europe, but all that changed on December 17, 1947, the 44th anniversary of Wilbur and Orville Wright's historic flight. An event took place at Boeing Field that ranks very near that famed accomplishment as one of the most important in aviation history. The event was the first flight of America's, and arguably the world's, first large swept-wing jet, the B-47 Stratojet. Seemingly forgotten in history, the Stratojet's revolutionary design was the first to pair swept wings with jet engines suspended from the wings in podded nacelles. Discovered in the Boeing High-Speed Wind Tunnel in 1945, this basic design is still the pattern for all jets built today by Boeing and Airbus.

Starting in 1944, a number of companies joined the competition to build the first U.S. production jet bomber. Douglas had been the first to fly a jet bomber with the XB-43. While it had the distinction of being the first American jet bomber, it was deemed unsuitable for production. Air Force requirements called for a 3,500-mile range, 45,000-foot service ceiling, and a top speed of 550 mph. North American Aviation's B-45 won the first round by virtue of being able to go quickly into production. Other competing planes included the Convair XB-46 and Martin XB-48. All of these airplanes followed the basic pattern for airplanes designed during World War II—straight wings with engines mounted on the wing.

Engineers at Boeing knew they could build a better plane. They also knew it would take a radical leap in airplane design to overtake the competition—that radical leap would be the discovery of swept wings and podded engines.

The swept wing came to Boeing in May 1945 by way of a hand-written letter sent from Germany by the company's leading aerodynamicist George Schairer, who was serving on Air Force General Hap Arnold's Scientific Advisory Group, which had been tasked with securing Nazi aircraft and rocket research. The data was also shared with other major manufacturers and did have an effect on other major designs, including the North American F-86 Sabre and Douglas F4D Skyray. Boeing engineers found dramatic results during wind tunnel tests of Schairer's swept-wing data, but they also discovered that the wings had to remain clean to achieve the high-speed benefits. This was a problem, since the standard design for multiengine airplanes was to mount the engines on the wings. The first solution was mounting the engines in the fuselage, but that idea was rejected because of the danger of an engine fire. The moment of discovery came to Boeing Chief Engineer Ed Wells. As he puzzled over the problem during a train ride back from Wright Field, Wells came up with the idea of engine pods that could be mounted off of the wings. The concept was tested in the Boeing Wind Tunnel by mounting model engine nacelles on the end of a pole (called the "broomstick" test) and moving the nacelles around the wing until the optimal position was discovered—forward and below the wing.

These discoveries came together in the Boeing Wind Tunnel as the optimal design for a subsonic jet and resulted in the revolutionary XB-47 that rolled out of Boeing Plant 2 on September 12, 1947—just two years after Schairer sent his note from Germany.

The B-47 design led to the B-52 and the 707 and is still the basic design for all subsonic jets in production today.

UNDER COVER. IN THE EARLY MORNING HOURS OF MARCH 15, 1952, UNDER COVER OF DARKNESS AND LITERALLY UNDER COVER, BEING COVERED IN SHEETS—THE SUPER-SECRET YB-52 IS ROLLED OUT OF BOEING PLANT 2 IN SEATTLE.

▲ Early jet engines had limited thrust, requiring the use of small rockets commonly called JATO (Jet-Assisted Takeoff) or more accurately, RATO (Rocket-Assisted Take-off) to achieve the extra thrust necessary to take off under certain conditions. Here the XB-47 demonstrates a RATO.

▲ A few early models of the B-47E retained the internal JATO system, but most B-47Es were built to carry a 33-rocket system that could be jettisoned after takeoff.

RECORD SETTING. THE XB-47 LEAVES BOEING WICHITA TO RETURN TO BOEING SEATTLE IN 1951. PREVIOUSLY, THE XB-47 HAD SET A TRANSCONTINENTAL SPEED RECORD, TRAVELING COAST TO COAST IN 3 HOURS AND 46 MINUTES.

▲ The transition from conventional straight-wing jets to swept-back-wing jets is illustrated well by these two contemporary North American jets; the XB-45 Tornado, which first flew March 17, 1947, and the XP-86 Sabre, which flew six-and-half months later on October 1.

America's first production jet bomber, the B-45, was a milestone airplane, but its role as a nuclear bomber was short-lived, being replaced by the B-47. The RB-45C, a photo-reconnaissance version similar to the B-45C pictured here, did carry on in the reconnaissance role until replaced by Douglas B-66s and Martin B-57s.

▲ North American B-45s are shown being assembled on America's first jet bomber production line located at the Douglas plant in Long Beach, California. The North American plant at Inglewood, California, was fully engaged in production of the P-86 Sabre. North American leased space in Long Beach from Douglas Aircraft.

⬆ Clockwise from top left. The Martin XB-48 competed against the B-47 and is an excellent example of what the conventional thinking was in airplane design at that time. Boeing borrowed the bicycle undercarriage from Martin.

The Douglas XB-43 was the first U.S. jet bomber. Making its first flight on May 17, 1946, it was quickly superseded by the North American B-45 and did not go into production.

These Boeing wind tunnel models represent the design evolution from the first concepts to the radical swept-wing podded-engine design. It was an amazing period of discovery and one of the most important in aviation history.

TOP SECRET. THE XB-52 SHOWS OFF ITS STEERABLE LANDING GEAR, ONE OF THE UNIQUE, AND AT THE TIME SECRET, ASPECTS OF THE B-52.

▲ The design team that developed the B-52 reenacting what has become known as the "Dayton Weekend." In October 1948, the Boeing team presented a turboprop design for the B-52 to Air Force Colonel Pete Warden, who suggested that the team redesign the airplane into a swept-wing all-jet design like the B-47. It was a Friday, and he gave the team until Monday to come up with a new design. Over the weekend, the team of (left to right) George Schairer, Vaughn Blumenthal, Maynard Pennell, Ed Wells, Art Carlson, and Bob Withington (not in the photo) worked on the new design. Schairer made a balsa wood model, and Ed Wells led the development of a 33-page proposal. After seeing the model and the proposal, Colonel Warden said, "Now we have an airplane; this is the B-52." After half a century, the model is preserved in the Boeing Archives, and the Air Force is still flying the B-52.

On April 15, 1952, the B-52 made its first flight. More than 60 years later, B-52s are still at the tip of the spear of U.S. combat forces.

The period between the end of World War II in 1945 and the fall of the Soviet Union in 1991 is known as the Cold War. One of the first acknowledgments of the Cold War was made by British Prime Minister Winston Churchill in a speech delivered on March 5, 1946, at Westminster College in Fulton, Missouri. In that speech, Churchill addressed Soviet expansionism in Europe and defined the battle line that existed between the Western democracies and the Soviet Union: "From Stettin in the Baltic to Trieste in the Adriatic, an iron curtain has descended across the Continent."

continued on page 100

STRATEGIC AIRPOWER

AIR COMMAND

▲ A Boeing KC-97A, the world's first production tanker, refuels a Boeing B-50D.

◀ Standing guard in front of a Strategic Air Command B-47E at March AFB in 1956.

AIR COMMAND

continued from page 99

In the early days of the Cold War, the United States concentrated its research and development efforts on airpower, including aviation and nuclear weapons technology. The resulting leadership in these technologies gave America a military edge over the Soviet Union and created a deterrent to any potential aggression.

The job of projecting airpower was the mission given to the U.S. Air Force Strategic Air Command (SAC), whose motto "Peace is our Profession" defined its role of deterring an attack on the United States through the promise of lethal and devastating nuclear retaliation.

SAC was an elite force that was equipped with the most advanced weapons in the world, many of which were designed and built by Boeing. When SAC was formed in March 1946, its primary weapon was the B-29. A year later, Boeing rolled out the advanced version of the B-29 known as the B-50, and Convair also contributed to the SAC inventory with the world's largest piston-powered bomber, the B-36, with the first airplanes delivered in August 1948.

Boeing was a pioneer in bringing jet power to aviation and soon presented the Air Force with the world's first swept-wing jet bomber—the B-47 Stratojet. The B-47 was fast enough to avoid interception, but it had limited range. SAC needed a plane with long range and jet speed. In response, Boeing designed the plane that would become a Cold War icon—the venerable B-52 Stratofortress. After 50 years, the B-52 continues to be a frontline combat airplane.

To give SAC bombers a true global reach, Boeing converted B-29s into flying gas stations called tankers. The first of these used a system of hoses to transfer fuel. In 1949, the KB-29 tankers made possible the world's first nonstop, around-the-world flight when the B-50A, the *Lucky Lady II*, made the flight in 94 hours, refueled in flight four times by KB-29s.

The system of looped hoses proved to be inefficient and exposed crewmembers to the elements. To remedy the situation, SAC asked Boeing to develop a more efficient system that could transfer fuel at a much higher rate and at higher altitudes.

Boeing engineers came up with the innovative concept of the "Flying Boom," a rigid, telescoping tube that extended out the back of the tanker aircraft. The flyable boom had small wings, or "ruddevators," that allowed an operator in the tail of the tanker to steer the refueling nozzle toward the aircraft requiring fuel.

The B-29 was also the first to employ the flying boom system, and between 1950 and 1951, 116 B-29s, designated KB-29Ps, were converted on the assembly line at the Boeing plant in Renton, Washington.

With the success of the innovative flying boom and the modified B-29s, Boeing went on to develop the world's first production aerial tanker—the KC-97 Stratotanker, and after proving the feasibility of jet bombers with the B-47 and B-52, Boeing went forward to develop a jet tanker for the Air Force—the KC-135 "Stratotanker."

Over its history, SAC used a number of Boeing airplanes, and their successes sprang from the outstanding relationship between Boeing and the USAF. It was the hard work of thousands of very talented and dedicated industry and Air Force leaders, engineers, machinists, ground crews, and flight crews, all of whom contributed to the SAC, that successfully fulfilled its mission of defending freedom, deterring aggression, and preventing nuclear war.

The U.S. strategy of containment and deterrence had allowed an even greater weapon to be employed—the ideals of freedom and democracy. Just as Churchill's speech had defined the beginning of the Cold War, a speech given by U.S. President Ronald Reagan on June 12, 1987, signaled that it was near its end. At the Brandenburg Gate, before the wall that split the city of Berlin between East and West, symbolic of the "iron curtain" that Churchill had described 40 years before, President Reagan said, "…I noticed words crudely spray-painted upon the wall, perhaps by a young Berliner: 'This wall will fall. Beliefs become reality.' Yes, across Europe, this wall will fall. For it cannot withstand faith; it cannot withstand truth. The wall cannot withstand freedom."

Two years after President Reagan's speech, the Berlin Wall was taken down, and on December 25, 1991, the USSR was officially dissolved, ending the Cold War.

On June 1, 1992, having fulfilled its mission, SAC was deactivated. The veterans who had served in SAC now have a new motto: "The Cold War didn't just end; it was WON!"

▲ Clockwise from top left. Cold War champions, Boeing President William Allen (left) and SAC Commander General Curtis E. LeMay: LeMay spent his career carrying forward the vision of Mitchell and Arnold. As the legendary leader of SAC, he built the command into a truly elite unit. Allen is recognized for leading America into the jet age. For his efforts, he was awarded the 1955 Collier Trophy for development of the B-52.

Boeing Wichita workers assemble B-47 tail sections. Except for the two XB-47s built in Seattle, all Boeing-built B-47s were assembled at the Boeing plant in Wichita, Kansas.

Following the team effort that helped win World War II, manufacturers teamed to build the B-47, including Douglas Aircraft, which built 274 at the Tulsa plant in Oklahoma.

Lockheed teamed with Boeing to build B-47s. In all, Lockheed built 385 B-47Es at the Marietta, Georgia, plant. The site had been home to Bell Aircraft production of Boeing B-29s during World War II.

▲ Birthplace of airpower: Boeing Wichita, 1957.

▲ The long reach: A KC-135A refuels a B-52D, giving the nuclear bomber the ability to reach any target anywhere on the globe.

⬥ Enduring value: Based on the longevity of both the KC-135 and the B-52, it could be argued that they represent one of the soundest investments ever made by the U.S. Government.

FRESH FROM THE FACTORY. A BOEING B-50D IS SHOWN ON A PRODUCTION TEST FLIGHT. THE B-50 WAS ONE OF THE PRIMARY BOMBERS OF THE STRATEGIC AIR COMMAND WHEN IT WAS FIRST FORMED. A MODIFICATION OF THE B-29 (ORIGINALLY CALLED THE B-29D), THE B-50 WAS UPGRADED WITH MORE POWERFUL PRATT & WHITNEY R-4360 ENGINES, GIVING THE AIRPLANE A 59 PERCENT INCREASE IN POWER OVER THE B-29. OTHER THAN THE LARGER ENGINE NACELLES, THE MAIN DISTINGUISHING FEATURE IS THE TALLER VERTICAL TAIL. THE TB-50H VERSION OF THE B-50 WAS THE FASTEST PISTON AIRPLANE BUILT BY BOEING, WITH A TOP SPEED OF 418 MPH—IN COMPARISON, THE TOP SPEED OF THE P-51D MUSTANG, ONE OF THE FASTEST PISTON-POWERED FIGHTERS OF WORLD WAR II, WAS 437 MPH.

▲ A B-47E moves into position to take on fuel from a KC-97.

A B-50D takes on fuel from a KB-29P.

SIX TURNIN'. THE CONVAIR B-36 PEACEMAKER, ALONG WITH THE B-29 AND B-50, WAS ONE OF THE FIRST BOMBERS TO SERVE SAC. NICKNAMED THE "ALUMINUM OVERCAST," THE B-36 WAS THE LARGEST PRODUCTION PISTON-POWERED BOMBER EVER BUILT. WHEN JET ENGINES WERE INTRODUCED, THEY WERE ADDED TO THE B-36, COMBINING THE ORIGINAL SIX-PISTON ENGINES WITH FOUR JET ENGINES MOUNTED IN THE SAME NACELLES DESIGNED FOR THE B-47 IN WHAT WAS COINED AS "SIX TURNIN' AND FOUR BURNIN'."

▲ An RB-52B just off the production line is shown at Boeing Plant 2 on Boeing Field in Seattle, where the famous B-17 had been built during World War II.

B-52Ds fill the flight line at Boeing Field in Seattle. Boeing Seattle built all early models of the B-52 through the B-52C and shared production of the B-52D, E, and F with Boeing Wichita. Wichita built all B-52G and H models.

▲ Clockwise from top left. Convair B-58s of the 43rd Strategic Wing at Carswell AFB, Texas, which was the first supersonic SAC wing.

B-47Es are shown at the ready at March AFB, California, in 1957. At the time, March AFB was the headquarters for SAC's 15th Air Force.

A B-47E from the 9th Bombardment Wing lands at March AFB. Bombers do not use thrust reversers like commercial jets; instead they rely on a drag chute to slow down after landing.

The first B-52H rolls out at Boeing Wichita. The H model was designed specifically as a "missile bomber," carrying four Douglas GAM-87A Skybolt ballistic missiles. First flown on March 6, 1961, the B-52H was quickly adapted to other weapons, including the AGM-28 Hound Dog missile, following the cancellation of the Skybolt.

▲ Boeing workers roll out their 1,000th B-47. The airplane is covered with donations from the employees to fight polio. Wichita built a total of 1,373 B-47s.

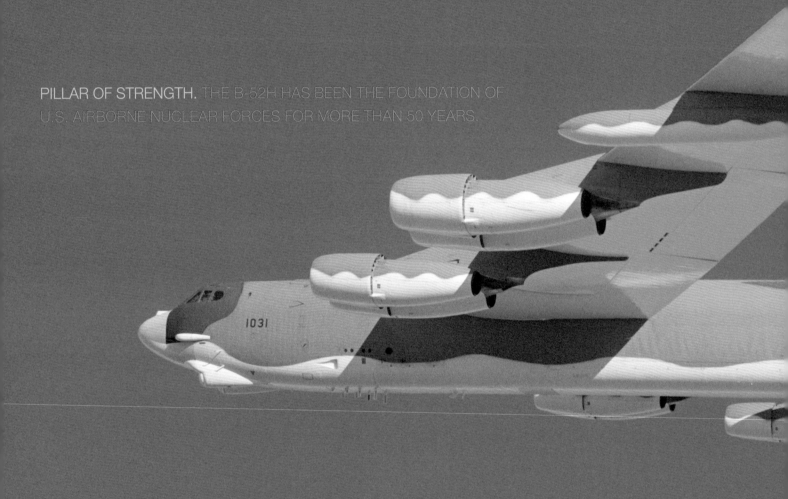

PILLAR OF STRENGTH. THE B-52H HAS BEEN THE FOUNDATION OF U.S. AIRBORNE NUCLEAR FORCES FOR MORE THAN 50 YEARS.

▲ Rockwell built 100 B-1Bs. First flown on October 1, 1984, the B-1B Lancer, or "Bone" (B-one), was designed to supplement the B-52 in the airborne leg of the U.S. nuclear triad. It could carry SRAM and ALCM missiles as well as free-fall nuclear bombs.

▲ The front office of a B-52.

NIGHT SPIRIT. AS THE LAST SAC BOMBER, THE NORTHROP/BOEING
B-2 SPIRIT "STEALTH BOMBER" CURRENT FLEET OF 20 PLANES, ALONG
WITH THE REMAINING B-52HS, NOW SERVE AS THE U.S. LONG-RANGE
NUCLEAR BOMBER FORCE.

One of the key
aspects of bomber
history is the role of
innovation. From all-
metal monoplanes
to swept-wing jets
and on to today's
radar-avoiding
stealth technology,
bombers have been
on the leading edge of
aerospace discovery.
Much like the
technological back-
and-forth between
RAF night bombers
and Germany's air
defense forces during
World War II, the rapid
advances in Soviet
air defense capability
drove continual
innovation in U.S.
bombers and strategic
systems throughout
the Cold War.

continued on page 124

INNOVATION

▲ A Boeing SRAM in final assembly at the Boeing Missile Production Center in Seattle, Washington.

◀ A masterpiece of innovative aircraft design, the XB-70 greatly advanced the technologies of aerodynamics and structures.

INNOVATION

continued from page 123

Early in their history, bombers depended on speed, altitude, and defense armament. With the advent of advanced radar and air defense missiles, bombers turned to electronic countermeasures to jam radar signals and stand off air suppression missiles to destroy air defense sites. Eventually, bombers had to rely on long-range cruise missiles to attack targets while remaining outside enemy air defense zones. Currently, low-observable and radar-avoiding "stealth" technology has become a key factor in bomber survivability.

Until the 1960s, one of the best defenses that a bomber had was speed, and the design for speed culminated in two highly advanced and very innovative designs—the Convair B-58 Hustler and the North American Aviation XB-70 Valkyrie.

First flown on November 11, 1956, the Convair B-58 Hustler has the distinction of being the world's first supersonic strategic bomber. During the 1950s, Convair was a leader in innovative aircraft design that combined the delta wing with the Coke bottle-shaped fuselage that followed the area rule principle discovered by NACA aerodynamicist Richard Whitcomb. Beautiful and fast, the Mach 2+ B-58 broke 12 world speed records, including the long-standing record for the longest supersonic flight set in 1963, flying 8,028 miles from Tokyo to London in 8 hours, 35 minutes, 20.4 seconds, with an average speed of 938 mph.

North American Aviation was a powerhouse of engineering innovation and scientific discovery, and it pushed the speed limit even farther with the hypersonic XB-70. NAA first flew the half-million-pound Valkyrie on September 21, 1964. The XB-70 had a top speed of Mach 3.08 and remains the largest and heaviest airplane to fly at more than three times the speed of sound.

Unfortunately for both of these airplanes and for the future of bombers at the time, advances in Soviet air defense and limited budgets resulted in just two B-70s being built and a short career for the B-58, which was phased out in January 1970, less than eight years after the last one rolled off the production line at Fort Worth, Texas.

After the B-58, the production line at Fort Worth would continue with the F-111 Aardvark, a medium-range strike interdiction aircraft and its strategic bomber version, the FB-111A. The FB-111A joined SAC in 1971, replacing the B-58. It supplemented the B-52, which would continue to soldier on, relying on advanced defensive avionics, decoys (such as the ADM-20 Quail), and long-range air defense suppression missiles such as the North American AGM-28A Hound Dog and, starting in 1971, the Boeing AGM-69A SRAM (Short-Range Attack Missile). The innovative SRAM guidance system permitted individually programmed flight, and the Mach 3 missile also had the capability of changing direction after launch. An FB-111 was armed with six SRAMs, and the B-52 could carry 20. Boeing delivered 1,500 nuclear-armed SRAMs, which remained in service until 1993.

The SRAM was effectively replaced by a follow-on missile also built by Boeing, the Air-Launched Cruise Missile (ALCM). In May 1980, Boeing was awarded an Air Force contract, and full-scale production of the long-range ALCM-B (AGM-86B) began. The B-52 can carry 20 ALCMs, with 12 externally on under-wing pylons and 8 more on a rotary launcher in its bomb bay.

One of the innovative features of the AGM-86B was its terrain-following ability. Using electronic data captured by a radar altimeter in its nose, the ALCM would make course corrections by comparing the radar with maps stored in its computer. The ALCM was upgraded to a Global Positioning System (GPS) guidance system when that technology became available. By October 1986, Boeing had built 1,715 AGM-86B missiles at its Kent Space Center facility in Kent, Washington.

Until 1986, the B-52 and FB-111s held up the manned bomber leg of the U.S. nuclear triad. At that time, the first of 100 Rockwell B-1Bs was built. Seen originally as interim to bridge the B-52 and the B-2, the B-1B was meant to revive the manned bomber threat by taking advantage of low-level flight and new stealth technologies that reduced the radar signature of the airplane.

Currently, low-observable technology, or "stealth," is the defense for strategic bombers and other airplanes that need to penetrate a heavily defended airspace. Much of the pioneering work behind stealth technology was initiated by the legendary Clarence "Kelly" S. Johnson and his team at the famous Lockheed Skunk Works ® during the development of the U-2, A-12, SR-71, and through to the F-117 Nighthawk "Stealth Fighter."

The latest U.S. strategic bomber, the Northrop/Boeing B-2 Spirit "Stealth Bomber," uses a number of stealth technologies to avoid detection, with one of the most important being its innovative tailless flying wing design. The B-2 first flew on July 17, 1989. Unfortunately, because of the extreme costs of the program, the B-2 became highly controversial, and only 21 were built.

With the end of the Cold War, the technology race between the free world and the Soviet Union also ended, but the need to continue to innovate has not. Going forward, the challenge of a complex world rife with a myriad of threats and the political realities of limited budgets will be major factors in driving innovation in the designs of future bombers.

BUILT FOR SPEED. THE B-58 DID NOT HAVE AN INTERNAL WEAPONS BAY AND INSTEAD CARRIED FUEL AND A SINGLE NUCLEAR WEAPON IN A LARGE JETTISONABLE CENTERLINE POD. THE AIRPLANE ALSO HAD HARD POINTS ON THE LOWER FUSELAGE TO CARRY FOUR ADDITIONAL B43 OR B61 NUCLEAR WEAPONS.

▲ The FB-111A was a modified version of the F-111 that replaced the B-58 as a medium bomber in the Strategic Air Command's order of battle. This FB-111A carries four Boeing AGM-69A SRAMs.

▲ Clockwise from top left. On May 11, 1964, the XB-70A rolls out of the North American assembly building in Palmdale, California.

The B-58 was one of the few airplanes fast enough to stay with the XB-70 and served as a chase plane during high-speed flight-testing.

Only two XB-70s were built; one was lost in a mid-air collision, and the remaining airplane was transferred to NASA for continued supersonic research. It was delivered to the National Museum of the United States Air Force in February 1969.

The B-70 design team developed a highly innovative way to increase stability and lift during supersonic and hypersonic flight: the outer wings would fold down 65 degrees, trapping the airplane's shock wave to take advantage of "compression lift"—the lift generated from riding that shock wave. The B-70 was one of the most aerodynamically efficient airplanes ever designed.

⬆ The General Dynamics F-111 was a long-range strike interdiction airplane that first flew on December 21, 1964. It introduced the innovations of variable geometry "swing-wings" and terrain-following radar developed by North American Aviation's Autonetics Division.

⏶ Convair was famous for its beautiful delta wing designs, including the F-102 Delta Dagger, F-106 Delta Dart, F2Y Sea Dart, as well as the B-58 Hustler.

▲ A B-52G armed with North American AGM-28A Hound Dog missiles. Starting in 1963, the nuclear-armed Hound Dog gave the B-52 a standoff attack capability. The B-52 could use the missiles' turbojet engine for added thrust on takeoff, making the B-52 a 10-engine airplane.

▲ A B-52 could carry 20 SRAMs, six under each wing and eight in the bomb bay. The SRAMs would be used to knock out enemy air defenses ahead of the bomber to create a path for the bomber to reach its target. The missiles could also be used on other strategic targets.

△ A B-52G with a full load of AMG-86B Air-Launched Cruise Missiles (ALCM). The B-52 can carry 20 of the ALCMs, six under each wing and eight on a rotary launcher in the bomb bay.

▲ The McDonnell ADM-20 Quail missile was designed to mimic the B-52's radar and heat signature and act as a decoy for the bomber. The missile was operational between 1961 and 1978.

AFTERBURN. THE FOUR GE F101 AFTERBURNING TURBOFAN ENGINES OF THE B-1B PROVIDE MORE THAN 120,000 POUNDS OF THRUST. THE CORE OF THE F101 WAS USED AS THE BASIS FOR THE VERY SUCCESSFUL CFM-56 ENGINE USED ON THE BOEING 737.

▲ First flown on December 23, 1974, the North American Rockwell B-1A was a Mach 2+ bomber that relied on speed, defensive avionics, and a reduced radar cross section (1/100th that of a B-52) to penetrate enemy airspace. Four prototypes (shown above) were built, but the program was cancelled in June 1977.

▲ Soon after his election, President Ronald Reagan authorized a go-ahead for the B-1, and in January 1982 the Air Force ordered 100 B-1s, designated B-1B, and the four B-1A prototypes were revived for the new program.

▲ A Boeing rotary launcher loaded with eight SRAMs in the bomb bay of a B-52.

⏶ ALCMs being assembled at the Boeing Kent Space Center in Kent, Washington. For guidance, the missile originally used an innovative terrain-following system that compared the terrain the missile was flying over with maps stored in an onboard computer.

EVASIVE AIRCRAFT. LOCKHEED BUILT 59 F-117AS AND 5 YF-117 DEMONSTRATION AIRPLANES. FIRST FLIGHT WAS JUNE 18, 1981, AND THE PLANES WERE OPERATIONAL IN OCTOBER 1983 BUT WERE NOT REVEALED TO THE PUBLIC UNTIL 1988. THE NIGHTHAWK WAS RETIRED IN 2008.

⏶ In October 1994, the B-2 "Spirit of Washington" visited Boeing in Seattle, giving some of the 10,000 Boeing employees that worked on the program a chance to see the completed airplane for the first time.

The Boeing contribution to the B-2 included outboard wings, aft fuselage, fuel system, weapons delivery system, and landing gear. Work on the bomber furthered Boeing's leadership in advanced composite structures for airplanes.

The birth and early growth of U.S. strategic airpower was entirely directed at bringing war to an enemy's homeland, to eliminate every resource that contributes to the ability of that enemy to continue aggression— what is known as total war. As predicted by the early visionaries of airpower when total war was unleashed, as it was during World War II, long-range strategic bombers were indeed the decisive factor for victory.

continued on page 148

MODERN TEST

▲ A B-52D flies head-on over the Boeing plant in Wichita, Kansas.

◀ A B-52F refuels during testing of "Project South Bay" in 1964, which added under-wing pylons to carry conventional bombs. The B-52F was the first model of the B-52 to see combat.

MODERN TEST
continued from page 147

The success of America and its allies in both World War II and in the Cold War can be directly linked to the U.S. commitment to strategic airpower and specifically to long-range bombers. The decisive display of American airpower, exemplified by the Strategic Air Command and its direct descendant, the Global Strike Command, has deterred total war since the end of World War II.

Unfortunately, war and the importance of active deterrence remain constants in the human experience, and while total war has been restrained, limited, proxy, and asymmetric wars continue unabated.

Airpower, especially represented by bomber and strike airplanes, continues to be the decisive force in fighting these modern conflicts. A combination of long range, structural strength, and mission flexibility are invaluable in allowing planes built for the singular purpose of fighting nuclear war to be adapted and modified to fight a variety of conventional conflicts. This adaptability is best exemplified by the venerable B-52 Stratofortress. Because of its strong basic design, the B-52 has been able to receive constant upgrades and modifications over its 50+-year life span that have allowed it to carry everything from the X-15 to 70,000 pounds (32,000 kilograms) of bombs.

Originally designed to carry nuclear gravity bombs, it was modified to be able to carry conventional gravity bombs and eventually every weapon in the Air Force inventory, including the Harpoon antiship missile (finally fulfilling the role that Billy Mitchell worked so hard to demonstrate by sinking the *Ostfriesland*).

The B-52 has proven itself invaluable in a variety of conventional conflicts. During the Vietnam War, the B-52D became a workhorse for tactical operations. The asymmetric tactics of guerilla warfare used by the Viet Cong were countered with carpet-bombing that eliminated their jungle terrain advantage. In December 1972 during Operation Linebacker II, B-52Ds and Gs and F-111s switched back to a more strategic role and were unleashed on targets in North Vietnam in a maximum effort to bring an end to the war.

Twenty years later on January 16 to 17, 1991, the B-52 once again proved the value of long-range airpower. Flying from Barksdale AFB, Louisiana, B-52Gs launched Boeing AGM-86C conventional cruise missiles that, along with attacks by F-117 Nighthawks, took down Iraqi air defenses in the opening salvos of Operation Desert Storm. The 35-hour mission was at that time the longest combat mission in history.

Today, as the U.S. Air Force faces a broad range of mission requirements, the B-52H and the B-1B, in an amazing display of mission flexibility and adaptability, give conventional fire support to small units of U.S. soldiers who are fighting in locations that cannot be reached by other support units because of terrain or distance.

Loitering for hours above the battlefields of Southwest Asia, the bombers serve in the role of a long-range heavy-caliber sniper delivering, at a moment's notice, GPS-guided Boeing Joint Direct Attack Munitions (JDAM) bombs with pinpoint accuracy to knock out terrorist strong points in the mountains of Afghanistan.

Proven decisive in total war during World War II, the formidable power of the long-range bomber has proven to be crucial in modern conventional and asymmetric conflicts as well. The B-52, B-1B, and B-2 continue to validate the vision of Billy Mitchell, Hap Arnold, and Curtis LeMay; but to maintain the indomitable force that those pioneers created, the United States must continue its commitment to airpower and especially to the future of bombers.

▲ A B-52D undergoing modification at Boeing Wichita in 1966.

⤴ A B-52D in "Southeast Asia" camouflage taxis at the Boeing Wichita plant.

DYNAMIC ADDITION. THE B-52D WAS THE PRINCIPAL VERSION OF THE B-52 THAT OPERATED IN SOUTHEAST ASIA. MODIFIED FOR CONVENTIONAL WEAPONS, THESE B-52S COULD CARRY 42 750-POUND BOMBS IN THE BOMB BAY AND 12 UNDER EACH WING.

Fully loaded B-52Ds take off from Anderson AFB, Guam, on their way to targets in Vietnam.

▲ B-52Ds on the Wichita flight line in 1966 undergoing the "Big Belly" modification that increased the airplane's conventional bomb load by 57 percent.

ENTER THE DRAGON. B-52H "DRAGON'S INFERNO" FROM THE 419TH TEST SQUADRON, EDWARDS AFB.

▲ The F-111 was an outstanding long-range strike aircraft. One of its notable missions was Operation El Dorado Canyon on the night of April 15 to 16, 1986. In retaliation for Libyan terrorist attacks, in particular the bombing of a Berlin discotheque that injured 63 U.S. soldiers, 18 F-111Fs from their base at Royal Air Force Lakenheath, England, along with four EF-111 Raven electronic jamming aircraft from RAF Upper Heyford, England, flew a 13-hour mission to attack military targets in Libya.